For the cub in every bear and little

THE LEGENDS OF 10

A BEDTIME BEAR STORY

written and illustrated by
ROY ADORJAN

Copyright © Roy Adorjan
Algonquin, Il USA
info@rnrairbrushing.com

www.RNRairbrushing.com
www.minimartians.com

Printed and bound in the United States of America
First printing

All rights reserved. No part of this book may be reproduced or transmitted in any form or by any means, electronic or mechanical, including photocopying, recording or by an information storage and retrieval system-except by a reviewer who may quote brief passages in a review to be printed in a magazine, newspaper or on the web-without permission in writing from the publisher.

© Roy Adorjan

Dedicated to my brothers and baseball

But, this is a tale
Of a century since.
That starts with a Rickett
And ends with a twist.

Come mid-season
They did not yield.
The pitching? Near perfect!
And, an All Star infield.

Things got even better
When Chappy was on board
Grrizzo and BearBryant
Continued to score.

The Cardinals would crumble
The Pirates would fade.
The division was won
With a GrandPaw Ross serenade!

Then the playoffs began
And the pitchers could hit!
Bear Baez would dazzle
With his defense and picks!

Game four was amazing!
All along for the ride
Contrerbear would tie it!
Chappy struck out the side!

They were finally back
Not since nineteen forty five.
In the world series
And with one BIG surprise...

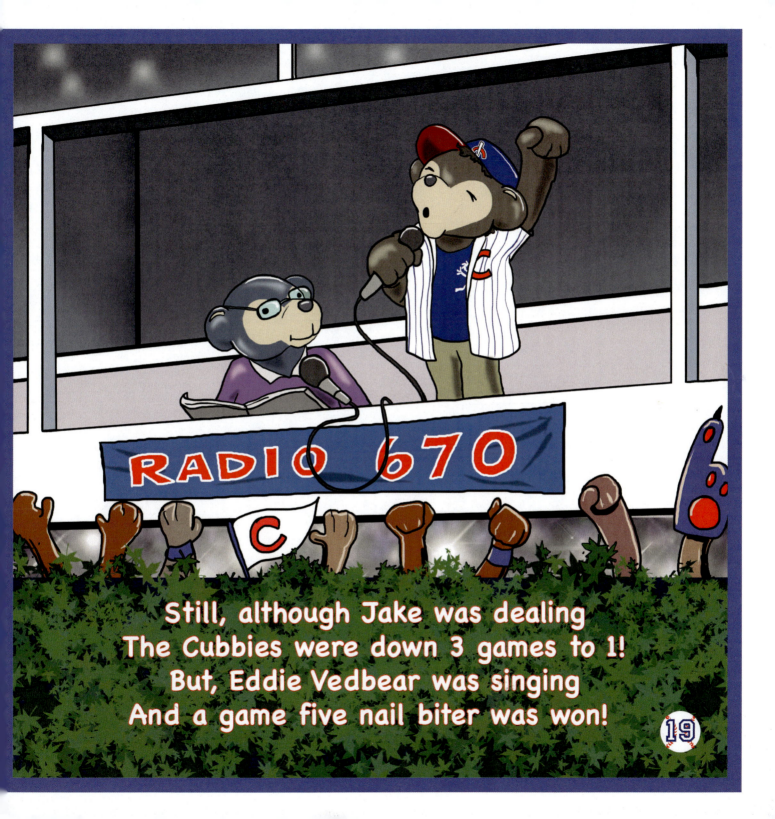

Game seven turned epic
With history at stake
Fowlbear would homer!
A quick three crossed home plate!

Yet, things would get scary
In the eighth it was tied!
And, as fate would have it
Rain fell from the sky...

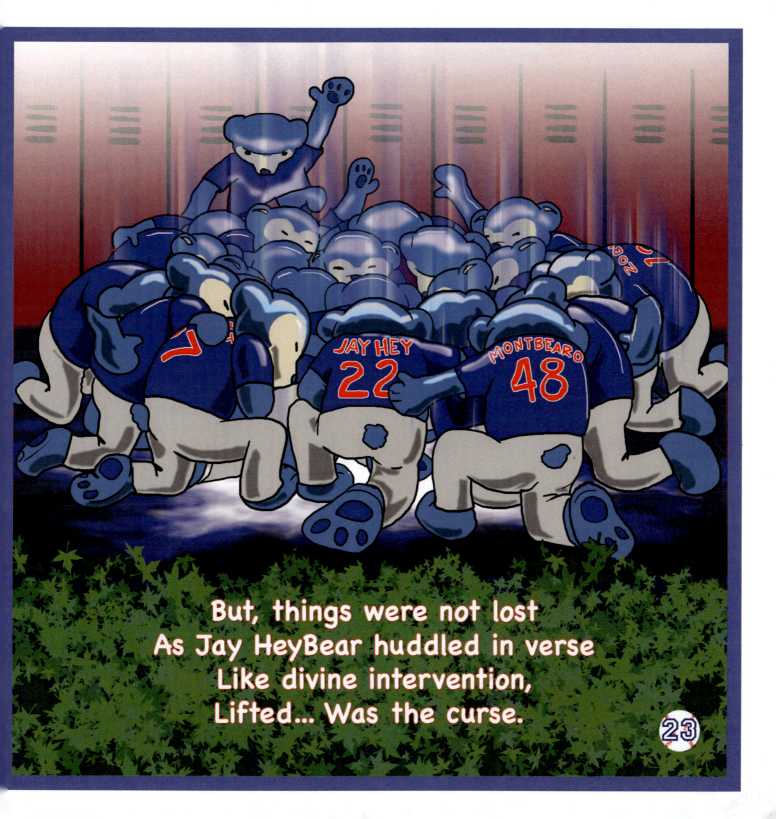

Neither Cardinals nor Mets
Not a Nat or a Giant
Through Dodgers and Indians
These Cubs were defiant.

The loveable losers
Are now the Legends of 16!

SEE YOU NEXT YEAR

Made in the USA
Middletown, DE
30 March 2023